A journey through

THE LAKE DISTRICT

Lo! the dwindled woods and meadows!
What a vast abyss is there!
Lo! the clouds, the solemn shadows,
And the glistenings – heavenly fair!

William Wordsworth

The dramatic Lake District landscape of lakes, waterfalls, fells and mountains was immortalised by Wordsworth, and has been the inspiration of poets, painters and writers from Ruskin and Coleridge to Beatrix Potter and Melvyn Bragg. The unique allure of England's only mountain region, with its powerful romantic associations, attracts thousands of visitors every year. How different from Wordsworth's day, when a coach passing on the road to Grasmere in the early 1800s was noteworthy enough for his sister Dorothy to record in her journal!

The need to protect the area's unique natural heritage was recognised in 1951, when the Lake District became the largest of the National Parks, covering an area of 2,279 square kilometres. Within it are some of Britain's highest mountains – Scafell Pike, Scafell, Helvellyn and Skiddaw are all 900-metre-plus peaks, while Great Gable and many others top the 600 metres mark. The region is now a major holiday destination and a natural centre for outdoor pursuits like fell-walking, rock-climbing, windsurfing and sailing.

It was the Ice Age that largely sculpted the landscape. When the glaciers moved outwards from the central fells, they gouged the main valleys into U-shapes and left 'hanging valleys' high up on the sides, the basis for spectacular waterfalls. Also formed at this time were the depressions that later became the lakes and tarns.

From the central 'hub' of Great Gable/Scafell the lakes radiate outwards like the spokes of a wheel, as Wordsworth noted. Each has its own distinct character. Wast Water is the deepest and most awesome – its fierce, desolate beauty presents a striking contrast to the holiday atmosphere and pleasure boats of Windermere, or the

leafy seclusion of Loweswater.

It is this variety of mood which is the key to the Lake District's enduring appeal. Even from day to day there are subtle nuances in the landscape, as the lakes mirror the changing aspects of clouds, sky and mountains. As the year progresses the effect is even more dramatic. October sees the start of the bracken season, when the landscape is ablaze with bright sienna tints, the brown of oak leaves and the rich purples of hazel and birch. Spring brings the vivid green of the larch and hosts of wild daffodils, while summer is the time of colourful festivals and traditional events. Ancient rush-bearing ceremonies take place in many villages and there are numerous country shows and fairs to visit.

The Lake District undoubtedly has a rich historic heritage. Evidence of Bronze Age settlers can be seen at the mysterious stone circle at Castlerigg near Keswick, and later the Romans left their mark in places like the fort at Hardknott, high above Eskdale. The legacy of Norse invaders lives on in place names ending in '-thwaite' (clearing) and in the descriptions of physical features like gill, beck, tarn and force. Castles and fortified buildings (pele towers) are testimony to the centuries of border conflict in the region, while relics of traditional industries like mining, quarrying and bobbin-making can be found in many museums. One survivor from Eskdale's granite-quarrying days is the narrow-gauge Ravenglass and Eskdale Railway, now a popular tourist attraction.

The Lake District's freedom and beauty, unique lake and mountain scenery and abundance of history have attracted visitors since the eighteenth century. It only takes a brief journey around some of its unforgettable sights, captured in these pages, to see why.

1 Fell Foot, Little Langdale

THE SOUTHERN LAKE DISTRICT

The 'auld grey town' of Kendal is the southern gateway to the Lake District National Park, and is famed for its characteristic limestone buildings, ruined castle and mint cake. The first glimpse of a lake from this direction is of Windermere, England's longest at 10½ miles. The Lake District National Park Centre at Brockhole lies just north of Windermere town and offers a wealth of information about the Lakes.

Past the major Lakeland centre of Ambleside lies the country most closely associated with William Wordsworth. At the tiny village of Rydal, where he lived towards the end of his life, a field has been planted with daffodils in his memory. At Grasmere the young poet found inspiration in the placid lake and surrounding hills, and composed his finest poems at picturesque Dove Cottage.

As well as literary landmarks, the southern Lake District offers spectacular scenery. For example, the footpath round the National Trust's Tarn Hows near Hawkshead gives panoramic views of Coniston Old Man, the Langdale Pikes and Helvellyn. The beautiful valleys of Great and Little Langdale are easily approached from Ambleside, with access to Skelwith Force and the delightful tarns at Loughrigg and Elterwater. There is history in the valleys too, where slate quarrying has been the main occupation for centuries. Evidence of a Stone Age axe 'factory' has been found at Pike of Stickle, while the peaceful village of Elterwater was once a gunpowder-making centre.

For nostalgia-lovers the Windermere Steamboat Museum, the Lakeside and Haverthwaite Railway and steam-powered cruises on Windermere and Coniston Water are thriving reminders of a bygone age.

2 Grasmere lake and island in winter

3 Abbot Hall in Kendal is one of the leading art galleries in the North West; it has recently been extensively refurbished

4 Kendal mint cake, enjoyed by generations of visitors, has also been taken on many world-famous climbing expeditions

6 The 'auld grey town' of Kendal from Castle Hill

5 The Museum of Lakeland Life and Industry at Kendal captures the flavour of bygone days, as in this authentic reconstruction of a chemist's shop

7 Sizergh Castle, just outside Kendal, is owned by the National Trust and contains an interesting collection of Stuart paintings and relics

8 A bird's-eye view of Windermere from Gummers How

9 The busy town of Windermere grew up after the arrival of the railway in 1847, merging with the neighbouring village of Bowness as hotels and other facilities were built to cater for the influx of tourists

10 A preserved steam locomotive on the Lakeside and Haverthwaite Railway, which terminates on Windermere's south-west shore

11 A tranquil evening scene at Waterhead on Windermere

12 Perhaps the best way to appreciate Windermere's attractions – islands, soft wooded shores and surrounding mountains – is by boat 'from the bosom of the lake', as Wordsworth recommended

13 The Windermere Steamboat Museum at Bowness-on-Windermere houses the finest collection of steamboats in the world. It features the nautical history of the lake from the eighteenth century, with steam, motor and sail boats on display

14 The lakeside at Bowness-on-Windermere, a busy base for traditional lake steamers, launches, waterbuses and cruises. Belle Isle, in the middle of the lake, features a famous eighteenth-century round house which is open to the public

15 Holker Hall lies to the south of Windermere and is a major Lakeland attraction, with museums and gardens to explore and various events taking place in the deer park

16, 17, 18 The World of Beatrix Potter Exhibition at Bowness-on-Windermere features the immortal Lakeland tales of Beatrix Potter in three dimensions using the latest sound and lighting techniques. There is also a programme of exhibitions and holiday events

19 Brockhole, the Lake District National Park Centre, lies halfway between Windermere and Ambleside in 30 acres of gardens and grounds. It offers various audio-visual presentations covering the area's geology, history and farming; there are also boat trips in the summer and various theme weeks

20 The tiny seventeenth-century Bridge House over Stock Ghyll, originally built as a summer-house, is undoubtedly Ambleside's most photographed building. It is now a National Trust information centre

22 Although many of Ambleside's buildings date from the Victorian era, it was in fact a communications centre as far back as Roman times and contains the remains of a fort built in AD 79. The historic town centre is a conservation area

23 Townend at Troutbeck is a fine example of a seventeenth-century yeoman farmer's house. Now in the care of the National Trust, it was occupied by the Browne family until 1944 and contains the family's original hand-carved furniture, domestic items and papers

21 Pleasure craft moored at the northern end of Windermere, near Ambleside

24 Rydal Mount was William Wordsworth's home from 1813 to his death in 1850. It contains interesting Wordsworth memorabilia and the gardens are still laid out in their original form

25 Every spring Dora's Field, behind Rydal Church, is ablaze with daffodils planted in the poet's memory

26 A colourful rush-bearing ceremony is held at Grasmere on the Saturday nearest 5 August each year. Children weave through the village, carrying flowers and rushes in traditional patterns, and lay them in St Oswald's Church in memory of the days when rushes covered the floor

27 Little has changed at Dove Cottage, Grasmere, since it was Wordsworth's home. Guided tours of the property are available, and manuscripts, paintings and special exhibitions are on display in the prize-winning Grasmere and Wordsworth Museum in the adjoining coach house

28 The village church at Grasmere, where Wordsworth is buried

29 Wordsworth called Grasmere 'the loveliest spot man hath found'; the placid lake and its surrounds provided a fertile source of inspiration for the poet

30 A peaceful view of Little Langdale Tarn, Wetherlam and Swirl How

31 The Langdale Pikes, seen here from Side Pike, are among the most easily recognisable mountains in the Lake District. Surging abruptly 609 metres above Great Langdale, they are an awesome presence in the valley

32 A panoramic winter view from the Langdale Pikes

33 An idyllic country scene, overlooked by the Langdale Pikes

34 Blea Tarn offers one of the loveliest views in the Lake District. The tranquillity of the tarn is offset to magical effect by the brooding silhouette of the distant Langdale Pikes

35 The name Elterwater derives from the Norse word *elptar* and means 'swan lake'; the lake still attracts Whooper swans from north-east Asia in winter

36 The combined waters of Great and Little Langdale surge through the narrow gap at Skelwith Force to fall 5 metres over a rocky ledge. The impressive waterfall and viewing platform can be found near Skelwith Bridge

37 Coniston Water is a natural centre for watersports such as windsurfing, as well as an ideal spot to go boating in delightful surroundings

38 A contrast to the bustle of Coniston Water: fishing at nearby Yewtree Tarn

39 The beautiful gardens at Brantwood, former home of the nineteenth-century poet, artist and critic John Ruskin. He bought the property unseen, believing that 'any place opposite Coniston Old Man *must* be beautiful'. The house and gardens are open to the public

40 The *Gondola* is a restored 1859 steam launch which runs scheduled trips on Coniston Water for visitors

41 The picture-postcard village of Hawkshead, situated in the vale of Esthwaite and surrounded by fells, is named after a tenth-century Norseman called Haakr. Wordsworth attended the Old Grammar School here from 1779 to 1787. The fifteenth-century church of St Michael overlooks the village's pretty white-washed cottages, old inns, squares and narrow alleys

43 The village of Near Sawrey was the setting and inspiration for a number of Beatrix Potter's tales. She wrote many of her most famous stories at Hill Top, shown here, including the tales of Jemima Puddleduck and Samuel Whiskers. The farmhouse is now a museum

42 The beauty spot of Tarn Hows lies two miles north-west of Hawkshead. It is particularly spectacular in autumn, when bedecked in reds, golds and browns

THE WESTERN LAKE DISTRICT

The Ravenglass and Eskdale Railway, running between the west coast and Boot, is England's oldest narrow-gauge railway and an interesting way to approach the foot of Lakeland's highest hills, many of which lie in the west. Generations of climbers have taken up the challenge of their ascent; indeed, the churchyard memorials at the remote hamlet of Wasdale Head are a testimony to the fatal attraction of the surrounding peaks. The Wasdale valley epitomises the Lake District landscape – here, England's highest mountain, Scafell Pike, overlooks Wast Water, the country's deepest lake, and the view from the northern shore of the lake towards Great Gable has been adopted as the National Park's emblem.

A Mecca for climbers, the western Lake District is also an oasis of peace and quiet. Many of its lakes, hills and hamlets are off the beaten track or inaccessible to cars. There is no road round Lakeland's most westerly and remote lake, Ennerdale Water, and tranquillity is guaranteed at Buttermere and Crummock Water, where power boats are prohibited. Wood-fringed Loweswater, owned by the National Trust, is a favourite haunt for waterfowl.

In contrast the Eskdale and Duddon valleys have no lakes but contain an abundance of crystal-clear streams and beautiful banks, making them two of western Lakeland's most scenic spots. Other attractions of the area include the coastal sand dunes at Ravenglass, home of colonies of black-headed gulls and terns; and the art treasures and world-famous gardens of Muncaster Castle, splendidly sited on the Esk estuary.

44 Wast Water, the deepest and most awesome of the Lakes, overlooked by Lingmell, Scafell Pike and Scafell

45 A major port until the Industrial Revolution, Ravenglass was a naval base in Roman times and the impressive remains of the Bath House, or Walls Castle as it is known, may still be seen

46 Situated one mile east of Ravenglass, Muncaster Castle incorporates a defensive pele tower erected in 1325, and contains a fine collection of furniture and paintings. The rhododendrons, azaleas and camellias in the gardens are world-renowned

47 The Ravenglass and Eskdale Railway was originally built in the nineteenth century to serve the mines of the Eskdale valley. Today, 'La'al Ratty', as it is affectionately known, is a popular tourist attraction and provides a regular service between Ravenglass and Dalegarth, near Boot

48 St Catherine's Church lies in an idyllic setting by the River Esk, 1/2 mile outside Boot village. Presumably it was built here to serve a wide area of both Eskdale and Wasdale, and yet still be accessible by riverside paths and stepping stones across the river

49 Guarding Hardknott Pass, the most dramatic pass in the Lake District with numerous 1-in-3 gradients and hairpin bends, is the Roman fort of Mediobogdum. It conforms to a typical Roman fort plan, being roughly square-shaped with gateways along each of the four walls, and headquarters building, commander's house, granaries and barracks inside

50 The long narrow valley of Eskdale stretches from the foot of Scafell Pike down to the coast at Ravenglass. Although it has no lake, it more than compensates with its gentle riverside meadows and attractive scenery

51 An industrial relic of Lakeland – a bobbin mill at Ulpha in Dunnerdale

52 The lush greenery of Dunnerdale Forest

53 The awesome profile of Slight Side and Scafell, seen here from upper Eskdale

54 Walkers negotiate the foot of Lord's Rake, Scafell

55 Wast Water is perhaps the most mysterious and dramatic of the Lakes; it is also the deepest in England at 78 metres. On its eastern shore dark and hostile-looking screes tumble headlong into the depths of the lake, while the dale head is framed in a classic Lake District view by the majestic peaks of Yewbarrow, Great Gable and Lingmell Fell

56 This picturesque old bridge remains from the time when the remote hamlet of Wasdale Head was on a major packhorse route.

57 The tiny church of St Olaf at Wasdale Head is well attended by climbers, who leave rows of boots outside during services

59 Climbers enjoy the view from the summit of Nape's Needle. There is an etching of the distinctive rock on one of the windows in St Olaf's at Wasdale Head

58 Great Gable rises up from the head of the Wasdale valley like a massive, steep-sided pyramid. It is prominent in all views from Wast Water

60 There is no road round Ennerdale Water, the most westerly and remote of the Lakes. Access by car ends at Bowness Knott, where there is a superb view of the lake and fells

62 Crummock Water shares the same glacial valley as Buttermere. Near the south shore is Scale Force, the highest waterfall in the Lake District, with a drop of 36 metres

61 The name Buttermere means 'lake by the dairy pastures'. One of the most beautiful of the smaller lakes, it can be reached via the Honister Pass from Keswick or Cockermouth

63 Loweswater is a small, relatively little-known lake north-west of Crummock Water. It is surrounded by softer, greener scenery than some of its larger neighbours

The Northern Lake District

Borrowdale's steep wooded hillsides backed by high crags and fells make it perhaps the most beautiful of Lakeland's dales, and prove that it is not necessary to scale great heights to enjoy spectacular views. It runs north from Seathwaite to the head of Derwent Water, the 'Queen of the Lakes'.

Bordering the lake's northern shore is Keswick, the capital of the northern Lake District. Once a market town and mining centre, it is now a popular tourist base for the surrounding lakes and mountains.

Among Keswick's local attractions are the scenic Lodore Falls, immortalised in verse by Robert Southey, one of many famous former residents of the town. Watendlath, a hanging valley east of Borrowdale, is also easily accessible from Keswick. It boasts one of the Lake District's best-known views – Skiddaw and Derwent Water from Ashness Bridge. Watendlath hamlet, which consists of a number of old farmhouses, has only comparatively recently been connected to mains electricity and its traditional character is preserved by the National Trust.

North-west of Keswick are Bassenthwaite Lake and St Bega's Church, inspiration for Tennyson's *Morte d'Arthur*. The poet was one of many literary visitors to Mirehouse, a nearby manor house, in the nineteenth century.

Further west lies Cockermouth, the birthplace of Wordsworth, and also of Fletcher Christian of *Mutiny on the Bounty* fame. The ancient market town occupies a strategic position at the junction of the rivers Derwent and Cocker, an advantage recognised by the Romans and later by the English, who built the castle here in the twelfth century to keep out the Scots.

64 Sunset near Blencathra

65 A solitary fisherman on the River Derwent in Borrowdale

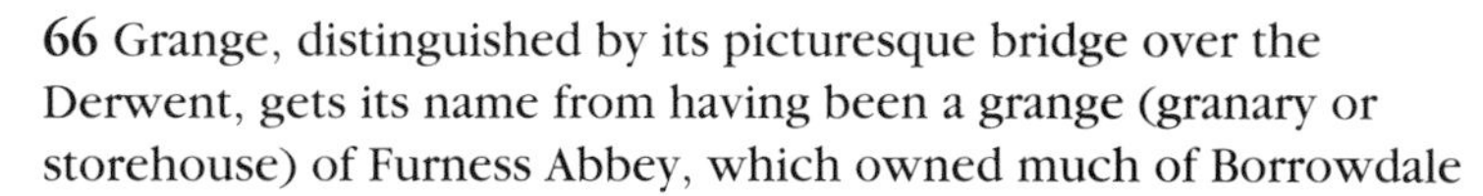

66 Grange, distinguished by its picturesque bridge over the Derwent, gets its name from having been a grange (granary or storehouse) of Furness Abbey, which owned much of Borrowdale

67 Foxgloves in the beck in Honister Pass, with High Crag, High Stile and Red Pike beyond

68 The River Derwent in spring

69 South-east of Keswick, dramatically enclosed by mountains, is Castlerigg Stone Circle. It was probably erected around 1300 BC but its original significance is uncertain, which only enhances the power and mystery of the place.

70 Once a mining town, Keswick developed into a tourist centre with the coming of the railway in the nineteenth century. It is in a beautiful position between Skiddaw and Derwent Water, and is seen here from Hawes End

71 The church of St John in the Vale, near Keswick

72 The southern end of Derwent Water from 'Surprise View', a famous vantage point on a precarious ledge beyond Ashness Bridge

73 Lying between Bassenthwaite Lake and Borrowdale, Derwent Water is bordered by attractive wooded shores and high fells. It is overlooked here by Causey Pike. Boat trips round the lake provide an opportunity to view its four islands and the surrounding country

74 The graceful curved form of Skiddaw is viewed here from Whinlatter Pass, but is visible from all directions because of its isolation. It is believed to be the oldest mountain in the Lake District, formed before the Ice Age

75 The unspoilt hamlet of Watendlath, near Derwent Water

76 The spectacular view from Ashness Bridge towards Skiddaw across Derwent Water is perhaps one of the most famous in the Lake District, and is dramatically enhanced by the changing seasons

77 The interior of St Bega's Church, Bassenthwaite. Founded in the twelfth or thirteenth century, it stands in an isolated field near the lake shore and was restored last century

78 Bassenthwaite Lake and the unique church of St Bega were said to have inspired the Victorian poet Tennyson

79 Mirehouse, near Bassenthwaite Lake, is a seventeenth-century manor house containing portraits and manuscripts of three Poets Laureate: Southey, Wordsworth and Tennyson, all friends of the Speddings of Mirehouse in the last century

80 The house in Main Street, Cockermouth, where Wordsworth was born in 1770 is now owned by the National Trust and is open to the public. It has been faithfully restored and has a pleasant garden and terraced walk

81 Scenic waterfalls in Mungrisdale, east of Keswick

82 Blencathra, to use its Celtic name, or Saddleback, as it is known more prosaically, is one of the grandest mountains in the Lake District. Here, walkers on Halls Fell survey the emerald green fields and woodlands far below

THE EASTERN LAKE DISTRICT

he main lake here is Ullswater, considered by many to be ıe Lake District's most beautiful because of its dramatic ariety of scenery. It extends in three reaches from Pooley ridge in the north to Patterdale in the south. Gowbarrow 'ark, once the site of Wordsworth's famous daffodils, and ıira Force, one of the Lake District's most visited vaterfalls, are easily accessible from the road which skirts he western side of the lake.

Patterdale and Glenridding form the main centre for xploring the mountains which dominate the head of Jllswater. Place Fell lies to the east, Sunday Crag to the outh, and Helvellyn to the west. On a clear day, nearly every peak in the Lake District is visible from the summit of Helvellyn, long immortalised in legend and poetry and one of Cumbria's most climbed mountains.

Separating Ullswater from Haweswater is the magnificent High Street ridgeway, named after the Roman road which ran along the top. Lying on the eastern extremity of the Lake District, the Haweswater valley is still comparatively inaccessible; even now the area can only be reached by a narrow cul-de-sac lane which runs along the eastern side of the lake.

The ancient market town of Penrith lies north-east of Ullswater. It is best known for its historic castle and parish church, where the mysterious Giant's Grave can be found in the churchyard. Outside Shap, a small moorland village between Penrith and Kendal, are the interesting remains of an early thirteenth-century abbey, and the Thunder Stone, part of a prehistoric stone circle.

83 The romance of the Lakes – Ullswater framed by windblown larch, fells and woodland

84 The parish church of St Andrew in Penrith dates from 1722, although the west tower survives from an earlier building

85 A curiosity in the churchyard is the Giant's Grave, two stones 4.5 metres apart, said to mark the head and feet of Owen Caesarius, King of Cumbria between 920 and 937

86 The Gloucester Arms a
Penrith dates from 147
and is one of the oldest inn
in England. The arms o
Richard III can be seen ove
the entrance; he is said t
have stayed here onc

87 Thirteenth-century Brougham Castle lies south-east of Penrith on a grassy mound beside the River Eamont

88 Ullswater combines many of the features which make Lakeland scenery beautiful with its scale, dramatic play of light on water and variety of views, including oak meadows, steep fells, dense woodland and rocky shores

89 One of the Ullswater steamers at Howtown Pier

90 Winter tranquillity on Ullswater

91 Patterdale is a corruption of 'St Patrick's dale' and the village is supposedly named after the saint's visit in AD 540, when he was shipwrecked on Duddon Sands on the way to Ireland. The Patterdale Sheep Dog Trials are held in the village each Late Summer Bank Holiday

92 The secluded valley of Boredale, east of Ullswater

93 Striding Edge is perhaps the most exciting of all walkers' routes. Seen here from the summit of Helvellyn (950 metres), it looks like a razor's edge of rocks. The crags on the left plunge down steeply to Red Tarn

94 Glenridding, formerly a mining village, is now geared mainly to tourists. The Ullswater steamers run to Pooley Bridge from here

95 The natural lake of Haweswater and hamlet of Mardale Green were flooded by Manchester Corporation in 1940 to make the reservoir of Haweswater we see today. A road was built to the head of Mardale, giving easier access to the awesome grandeur of Harter Fell and the High Street range

96 The Kirkstone, in the Kirkstone Pass near Ullswater, is thought to resemble a church steeple. The road through the dramatic pass is the highest in the Lake District

97 Thirlmere is a reservoir created in 1890-92 by Manchester Corporation. Two smaller lakes, Leathe's Water and Wythburn Water, were joined up when the valley was flooded

98 A panoramic view of Swindale from Outlaw Crag, near Shap

99 The ruins of Shap Abbey lie outside Shap village. The abbey was one of the last to be dissolved by Henry VIII in 1540 because, it is said, of the shelter it afforded travellers crossing the wild Shap Fells

Text by Bernadette Sheehan
ISBN 0-7117-0596-8

Published by Jarrold Publishing, Norwich
Printed in Great Britain 2/97

Photo credits: A. Faulkner Taylor (**1**); Tom Parker (**2, 7, 11, 25, 33, 38, 39, 55, 65, 67, 68, 83, 87, 88, 91, 95, 98**); Abbot Hall Art Gallery, Kendal (**3, 5**); The World of Beatrix Potter Exhibition (**16, 17, 18**); Percy V. Jacobs (**22, 26, 30, 31, 44, 53, 54, 56, 58, 66, 69, 82, 93, 96**); F.L. Ideson (**32**); R. Dixon (**35, back cover**); J. Winkley (**61**); Raymond R. Holt (**74**); Lynda Freebrey (**78**).